CONTENTS

Pictionary – CVC Words with vowel "a"

MELS®

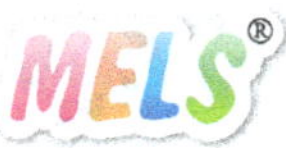

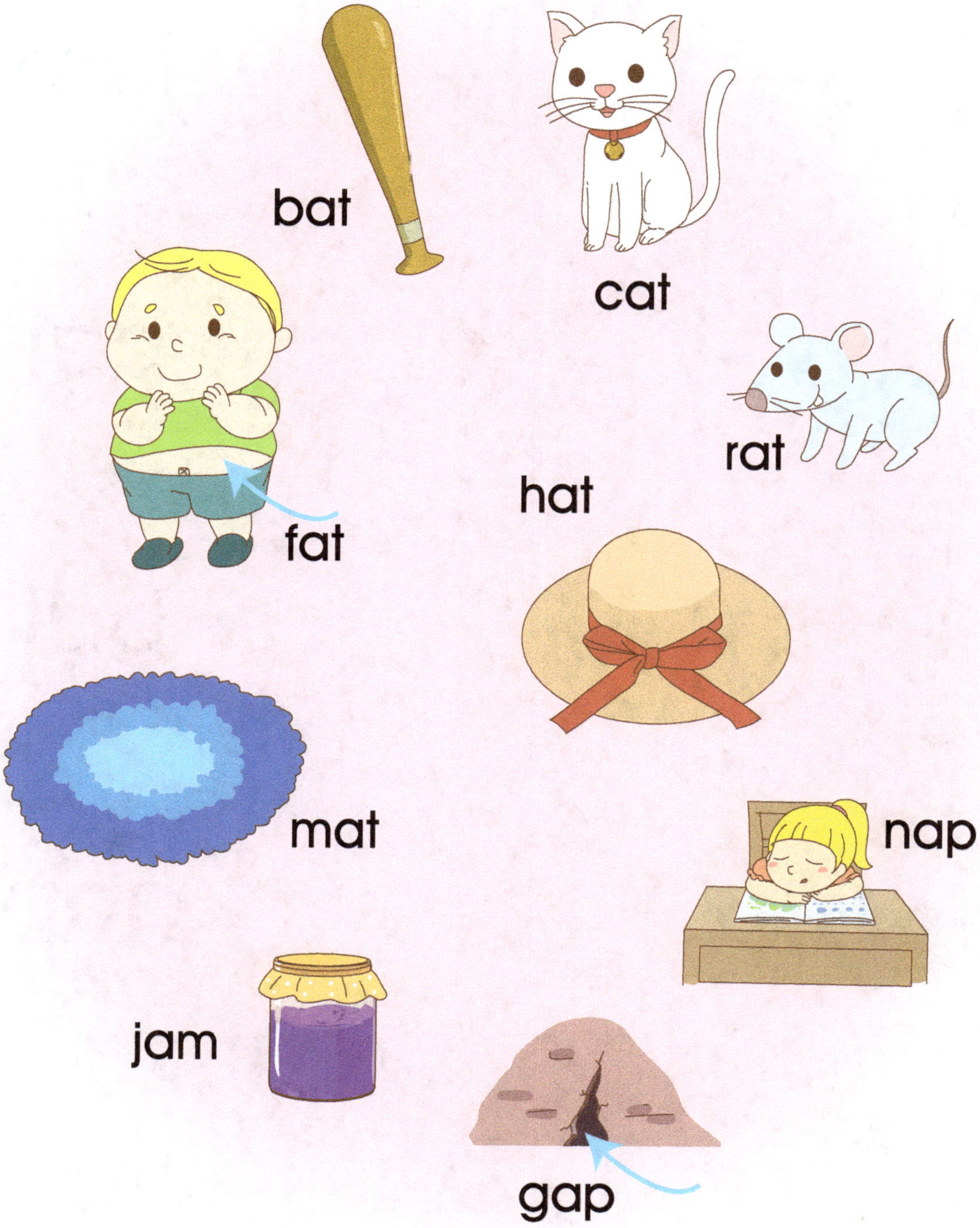
bat
cat
fat
rat
hat
mat
nap
jam
gap

Join the pictures to the words.

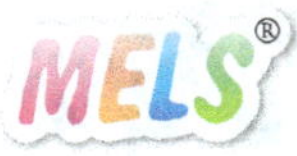

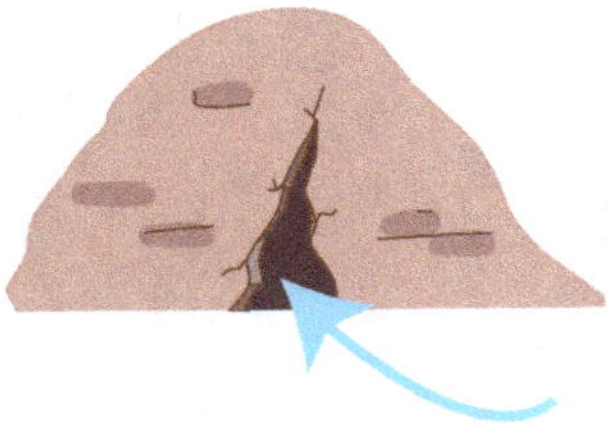

jam

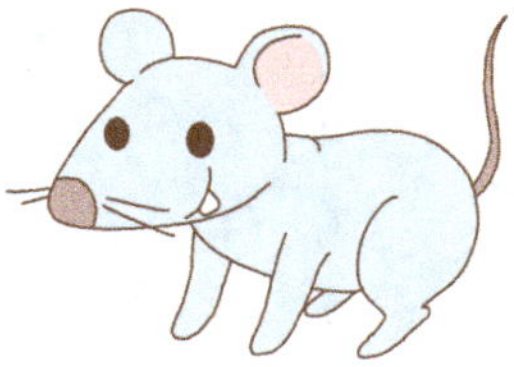

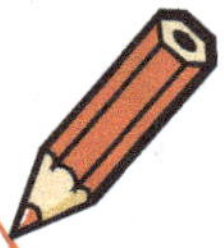

cat

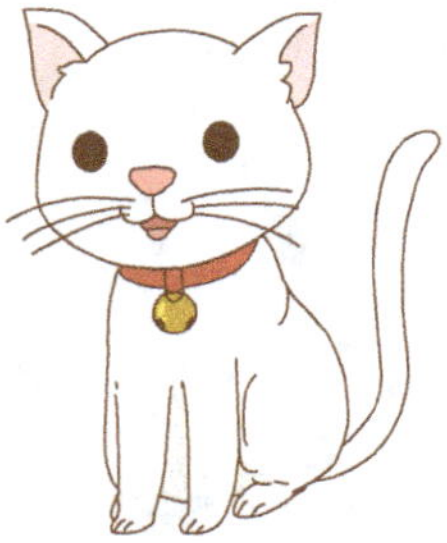

bat

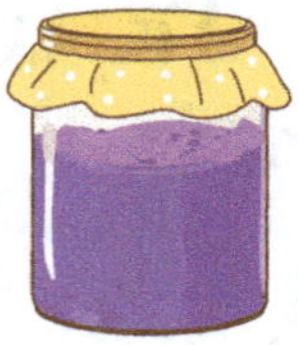

gap

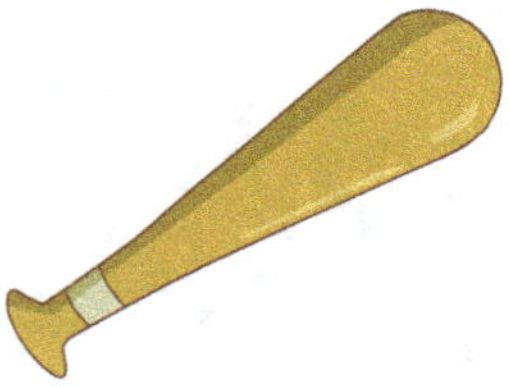

rat

hat

jam

cat

nap

gap

bat

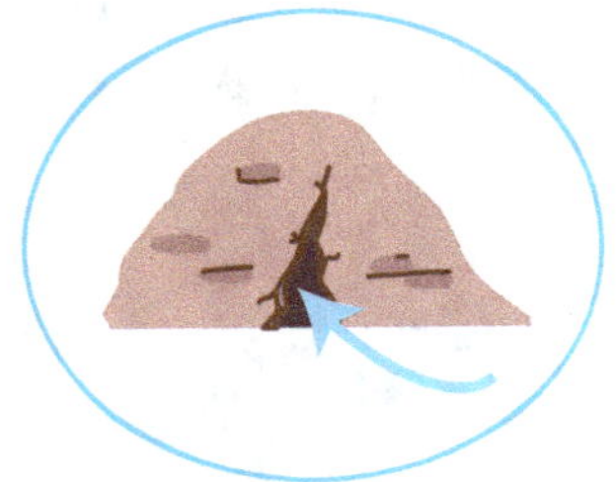

g l n

b c r

m h b

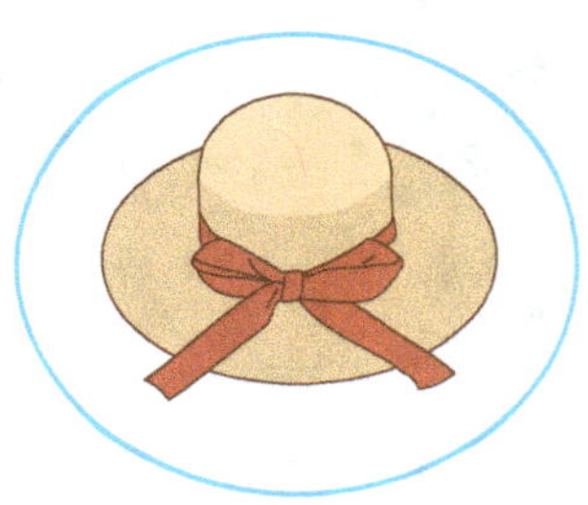

f h j

j   m

t   c

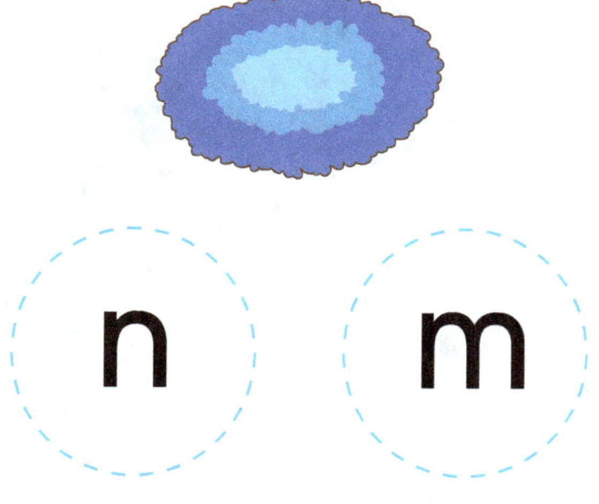

n   m

r   b

Match the **ending** sounds according to the pictures.

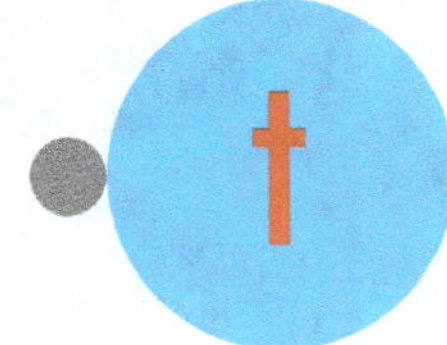

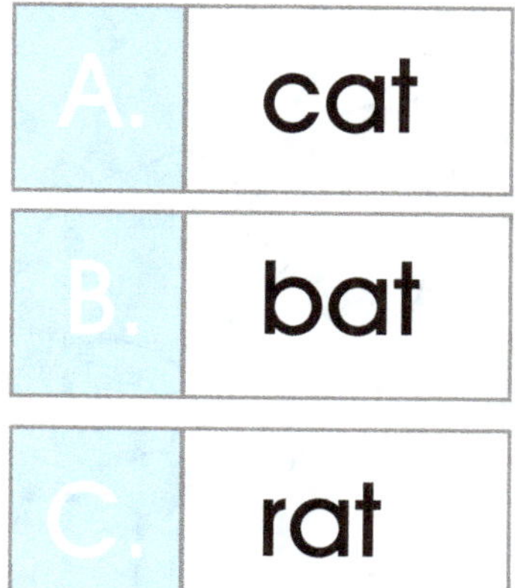

A.	cat
B.	bat
C.	rat

A.	fat
B.	rat
C.	mat

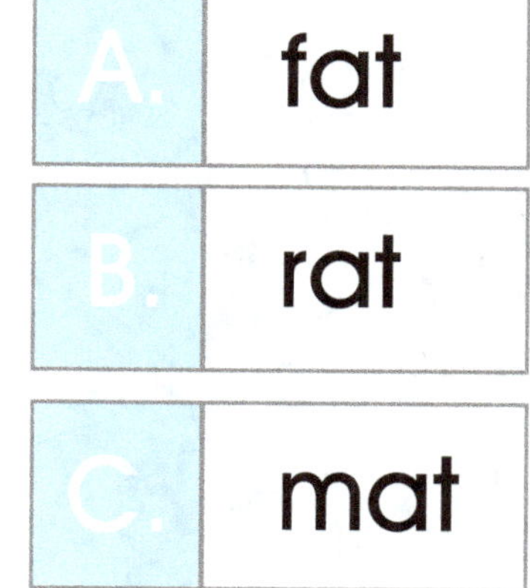

A.	fat
B.	rat
C.	cat

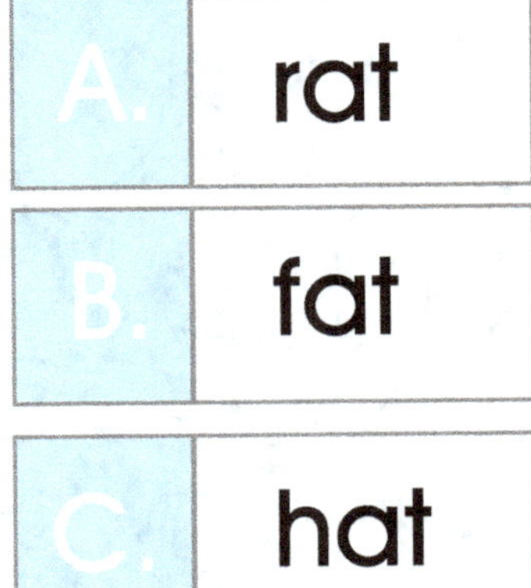

A.	rat
B.	fat
C.	hat

A.	mat
B.	bat
C.	fat

A.	mat
B.	bat
C.	rat

There are two cats outside the hut. The fat and the cat. They decide to go fishing.

.1.   .2.

There is a rat hiding behind the tree. He sees the fat and the cat leave the fish on the table.

.3.   .4.

The fat and the cat decide to go into the river to clean themselves. As they are away from the fish, the rat jumps onto the table.

.5.   .6.

Study the story carefully and answer the questions on page 11 & 12.

The plate drops and hits the ground. It is heard by the cat.

.7.

.8.

The cat is very angry. He wants to hit the rat with the bat.

.9.

.10.

The rat hides the food under the mat. When the cat arrives, he does not see the rat as the rat hides himself behind the hat.

.11.

.12.

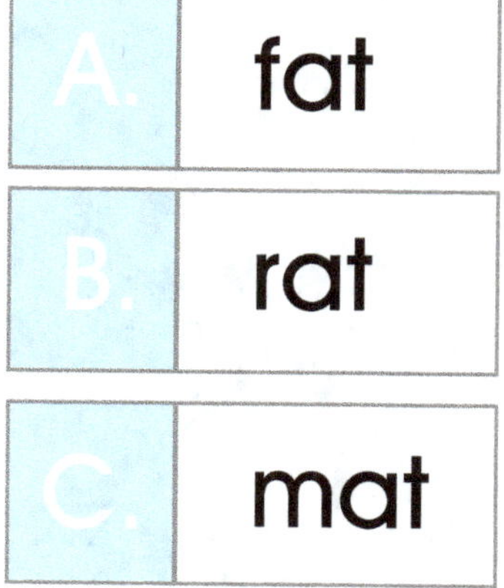

A.	fat
B.	rat
C.	mat

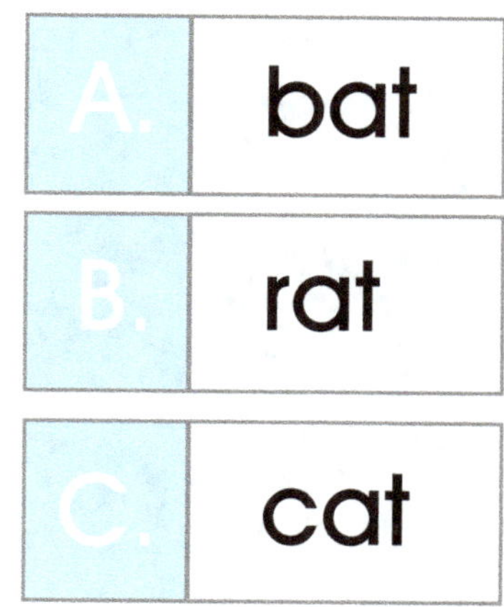

A.	bat
B.	rat
C.	cat

A.	cat
B.	bat
C.	rat

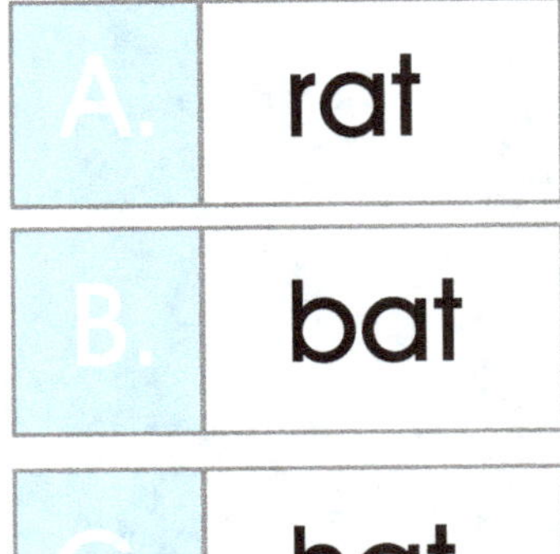

A. rat
B. bat
C. hat

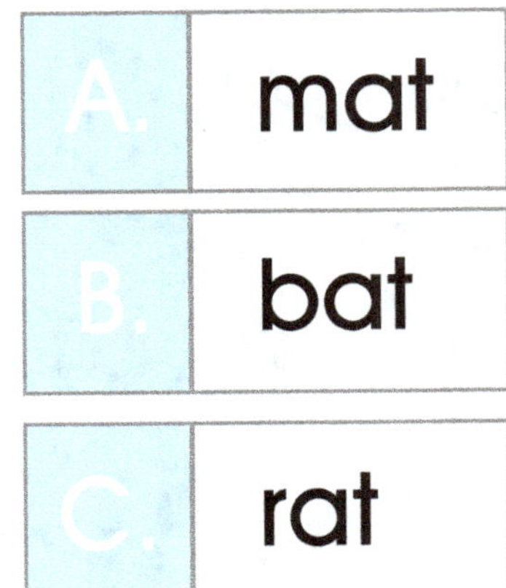

A. mat
B. bat
C. rat

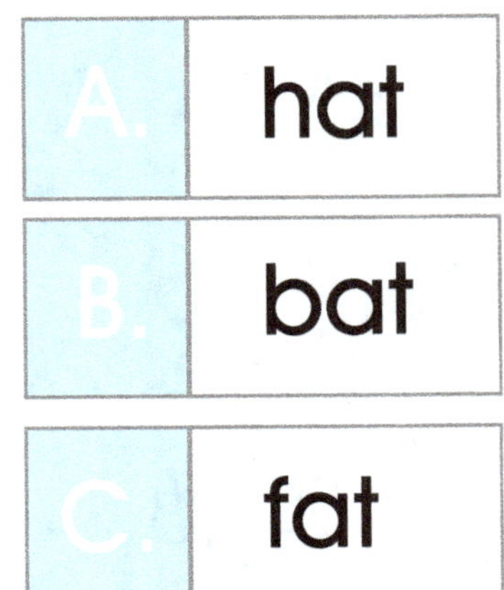

A. hat
B. bat
C. fat

The cat is on
the mat.

The bat is on
the mat.

The rat is on
the cat.

What is the rat doing?

The rat is sleeping on the mat.

The rat is eating the jam.

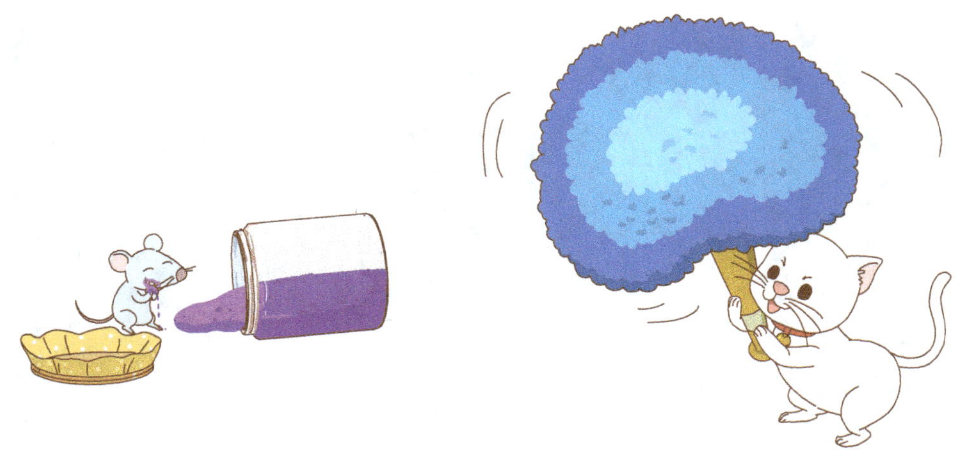

What is the cat doing?

The cat is playing with a bat and a mat.

The cat is wearing a hat.

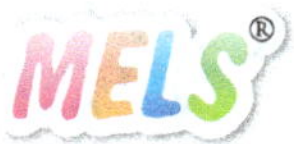

Pictionary – CVC Words with vowel "e"

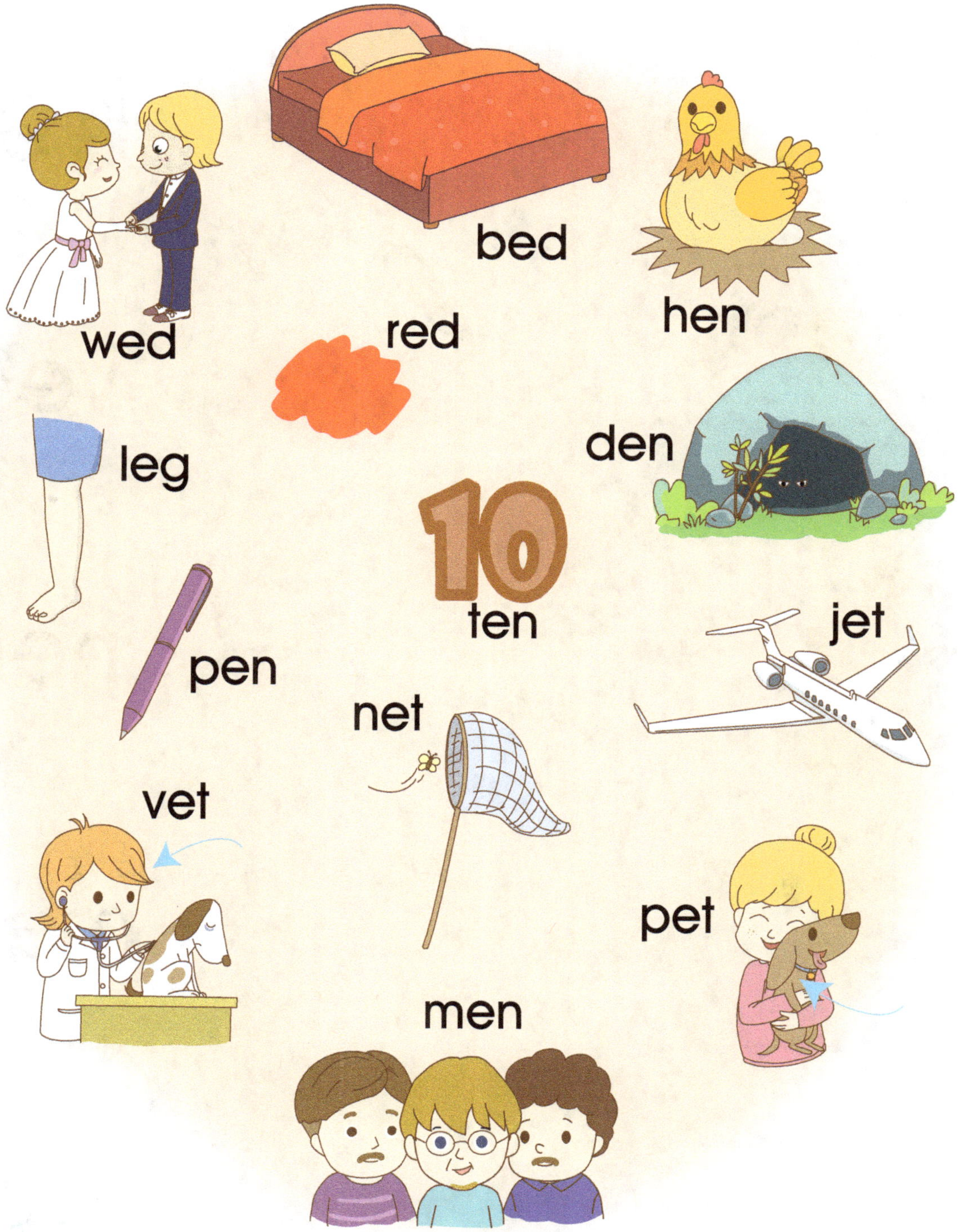
bed
wed
red
hen
den
leg
10
ten
jet
pen
net
vet
pet
men

Join the pictures to the words.

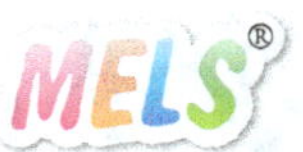

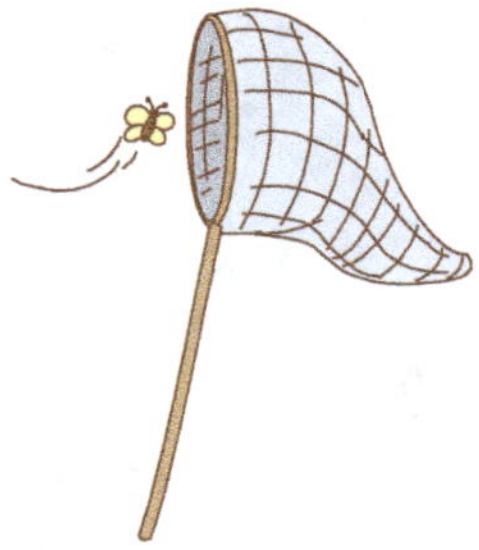

leg

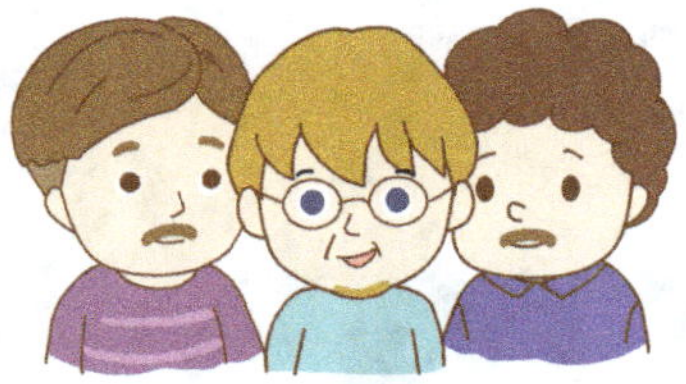

vet

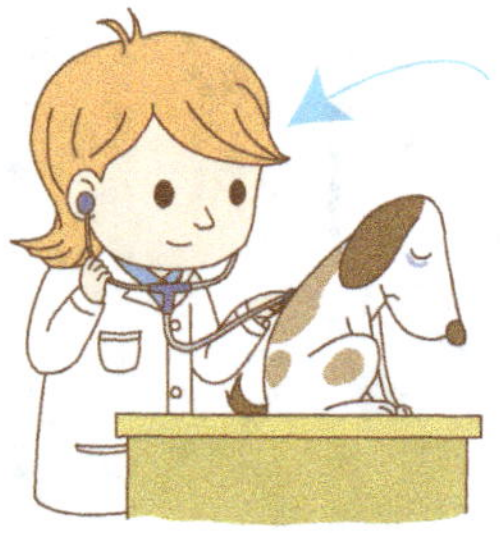

net

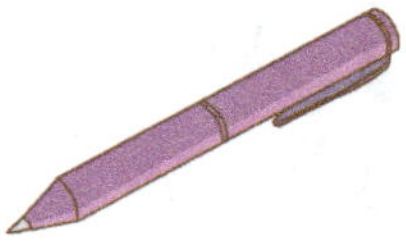

men

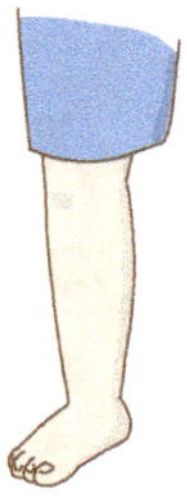

pen

Colour the correct words that match the pictures.

net   jet

wed   red

bed   vet

leg   ten

net   pet

men   hen

d •

v •

n •

r •

• __et 

• __ed 

• __et 

• __en 

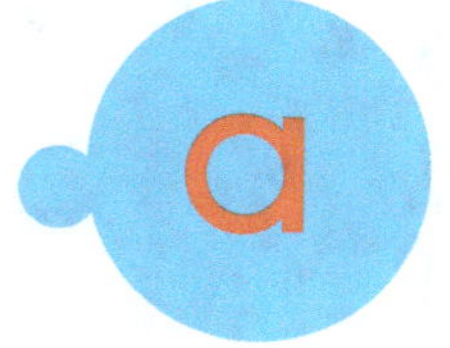

a

e

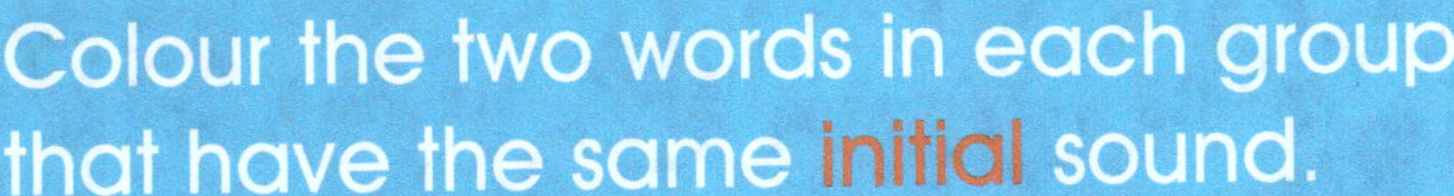

hen	bed	ten
red	bat	pen
hat	nap	fat
jet	vet	pet

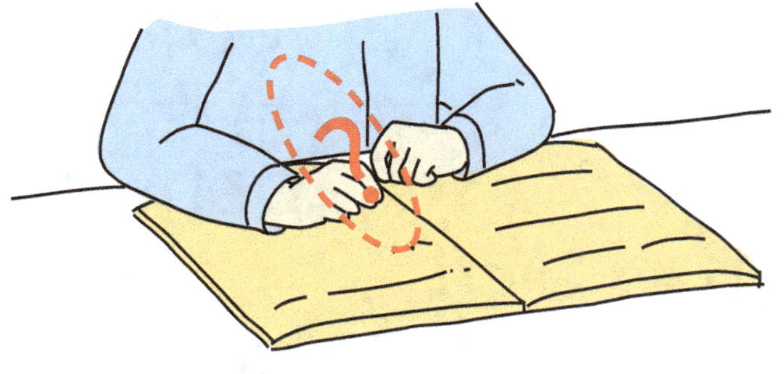

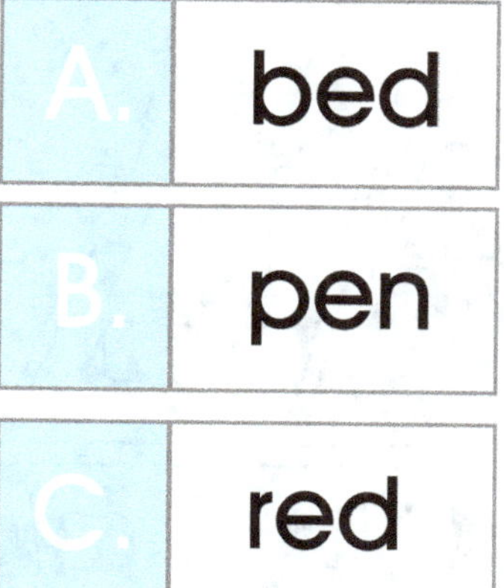

A.	bed
B.	pen
C.	red

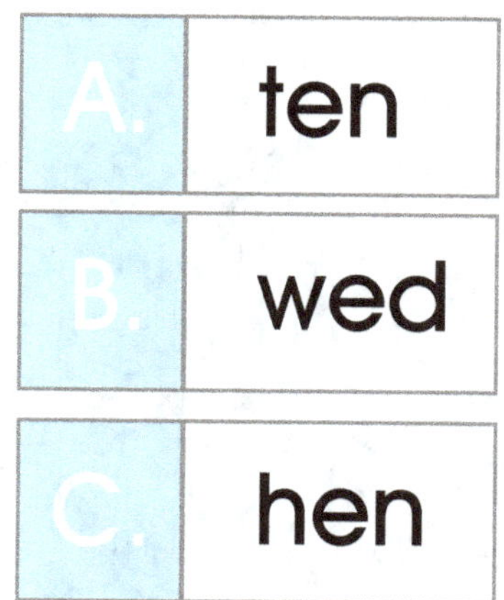

A.	ten
B.	wed
C.	hen

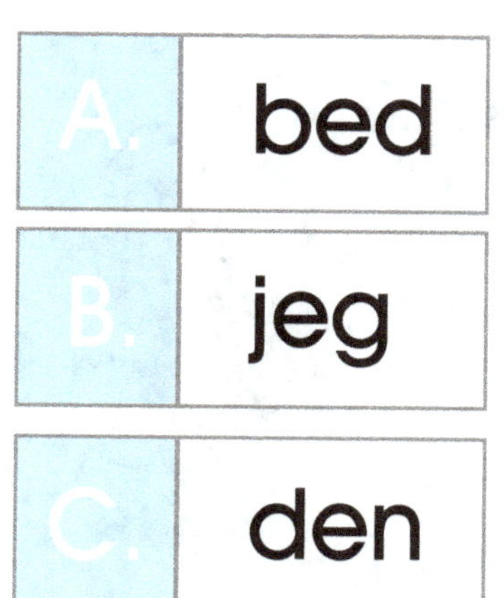

A.	bed
B.	jeg
C.	den

Guess the object inside ? . Circle the answers.

The colour of the traffic light is …

A.	red
B.	pen
C.	den

There is a ___ behind the lady.

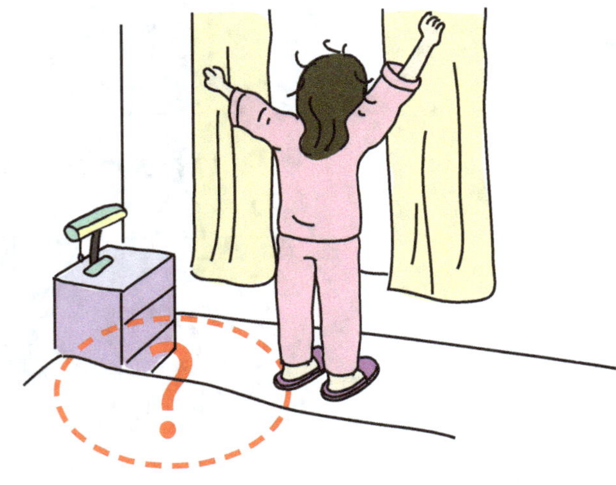

A.	wed
B.	red
C.	bed

This is a …

A.	ten
B.	hen
C.	bed

Ted writes in his diary before going to bed.

.1.

The next morning, as soon as he wakes up, he looks out of the window.

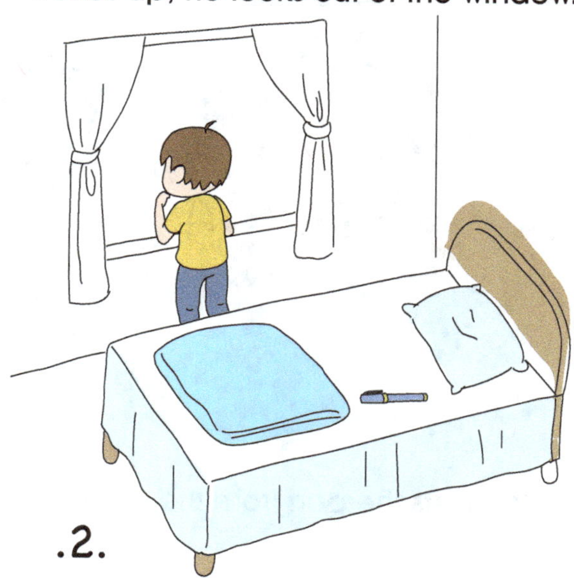

.2.

When he jogs along the river, he notices that there are some men outside the hut.

.3.

The ten men are looking at the red hen.

.4.

The man puts the cages on the truck.

.5.

Ted gets the pen from the man.

.6.

The men leave the hut in a truck.

.7.

The ....

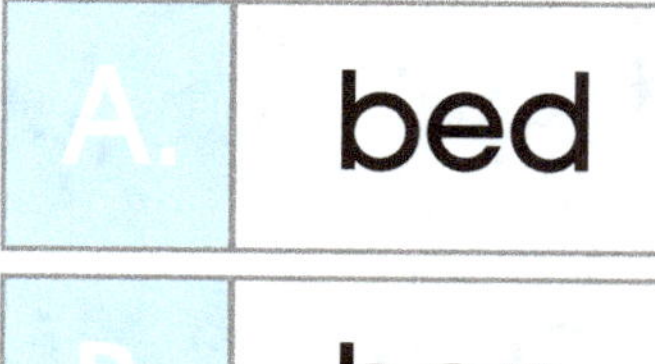

A.	bed
B.	hen
C.	men

The colour

A.	ten
B.	red
C.	pen

This is a ...

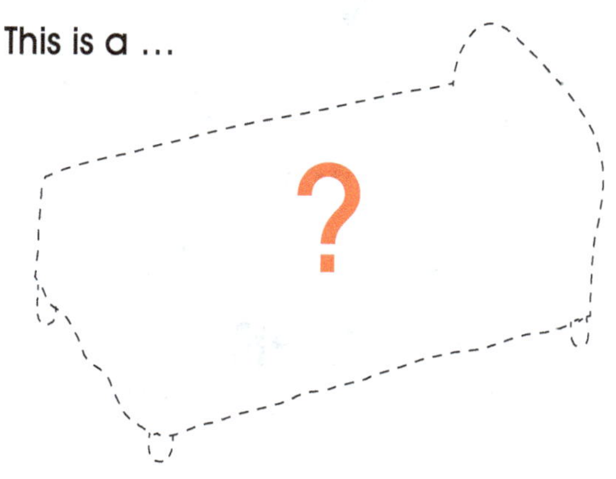

A.	pet
B.	den
C.	bed

I need a ...

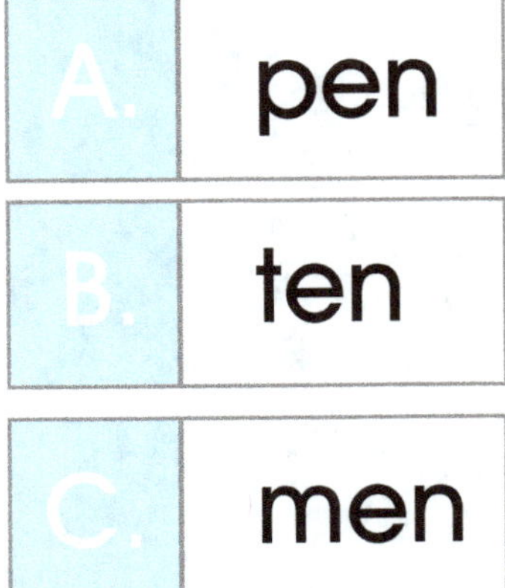

A.	pen
B.	ten
C.	men

10

A.	men
B.	pet
C.	ten

The ... is inside the cage.

A.	vet
B.	hen
C.	pen

The cat has a net.

The rat has a bed.

The hen has a pen.

What is the hen doing?

The hen is running out from a den.

The hen is playing in the den.

What do the men like?

The men like the fat hen.

The men like the red bed.

win

fin

tin

hit

bin

lid

pit

dig

wig

kid

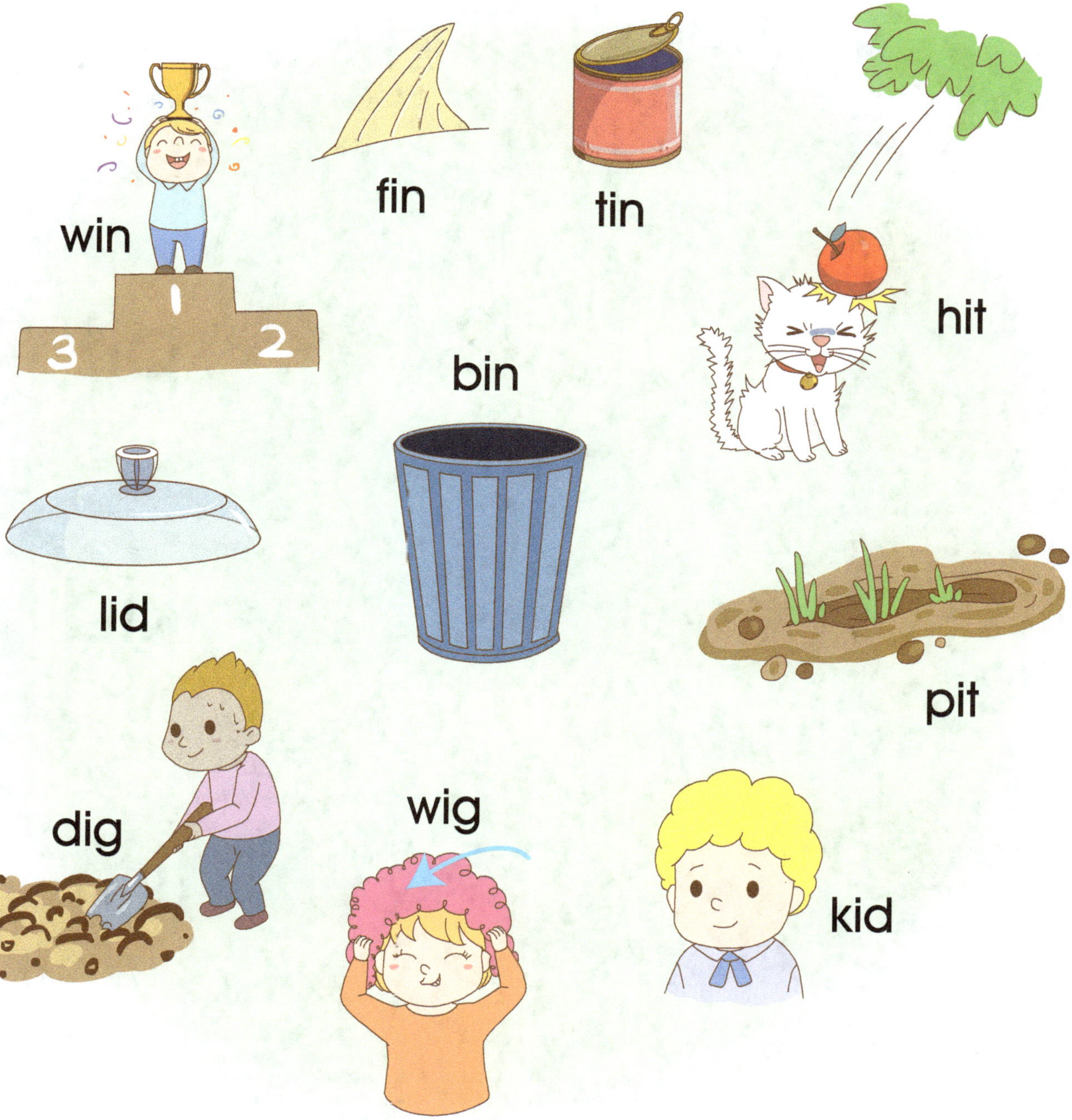

Join the pictures to the words.

MELS®

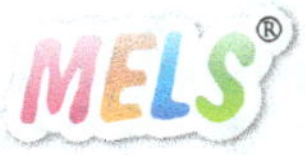

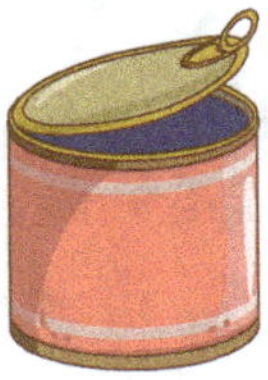

win

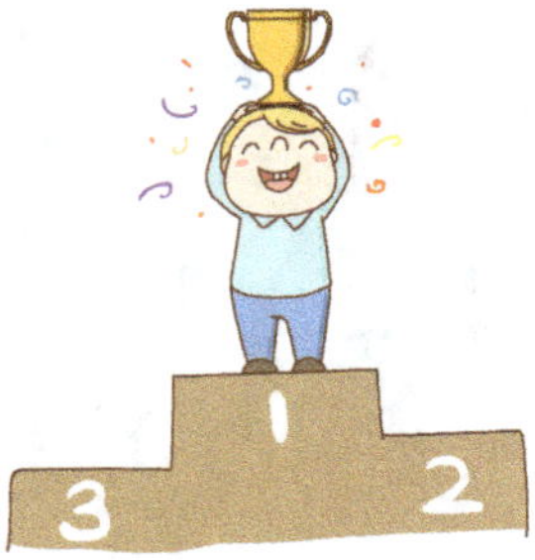

pit

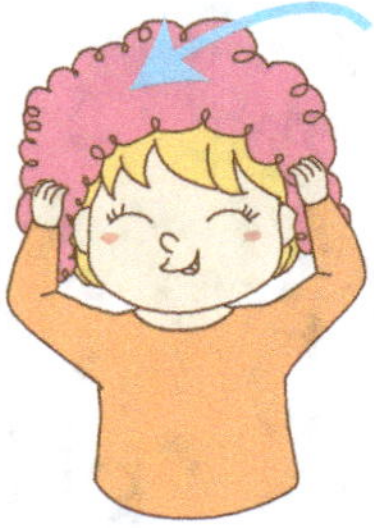

kid

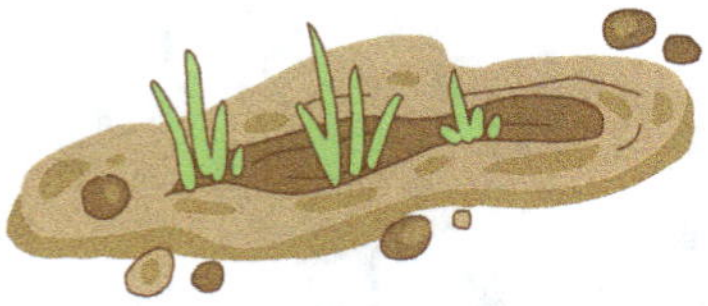

tin

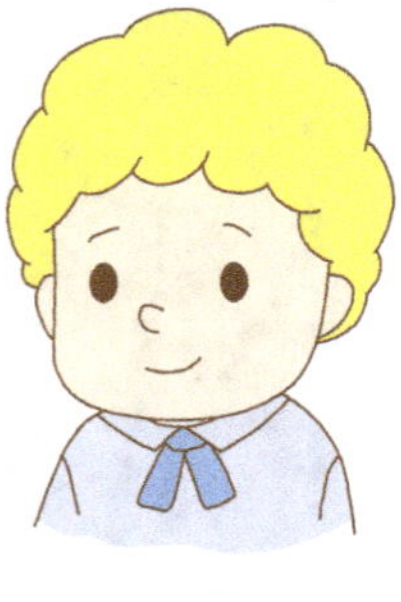

wig

Match the correct words to the pictures.

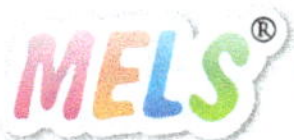

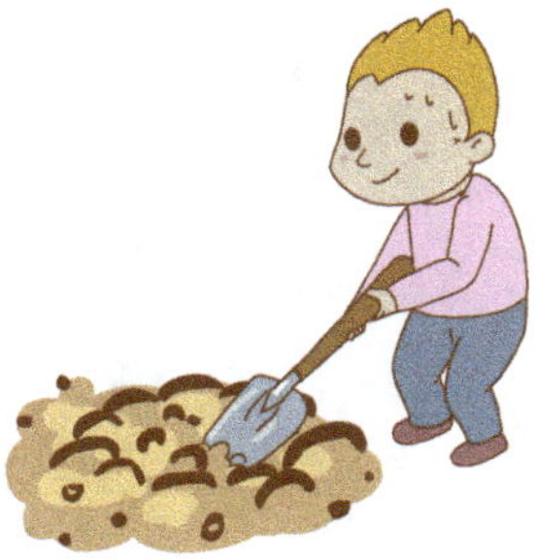

dig

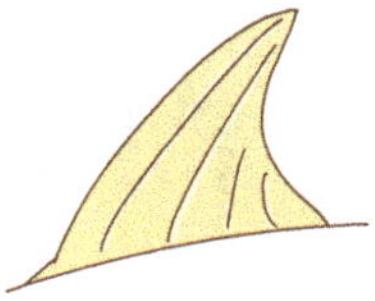

lid

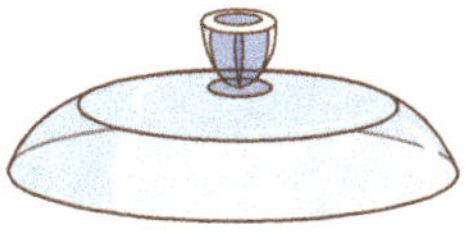

bin

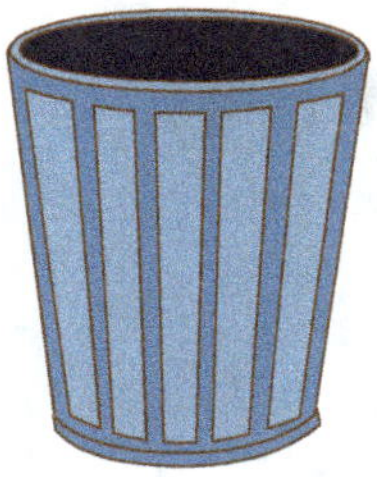

hit

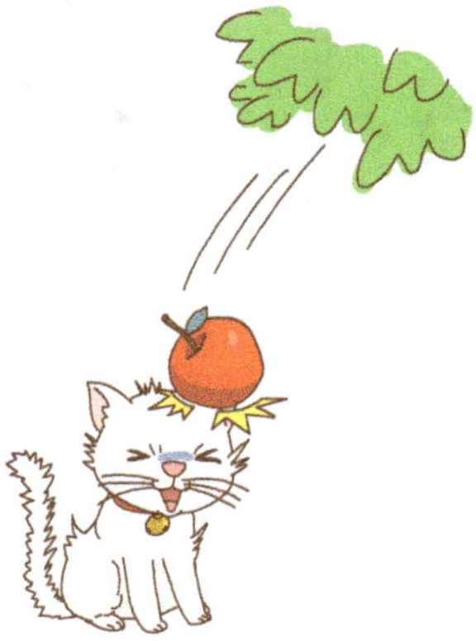

fin

h i t i n

t i p i n

g i w i g

k i d i g

vet

pan

hen

zip

hit

hat

Match the words on the left to the words on the right that have the same **ending** sound.

wed

wig

hen

lid

leg

win

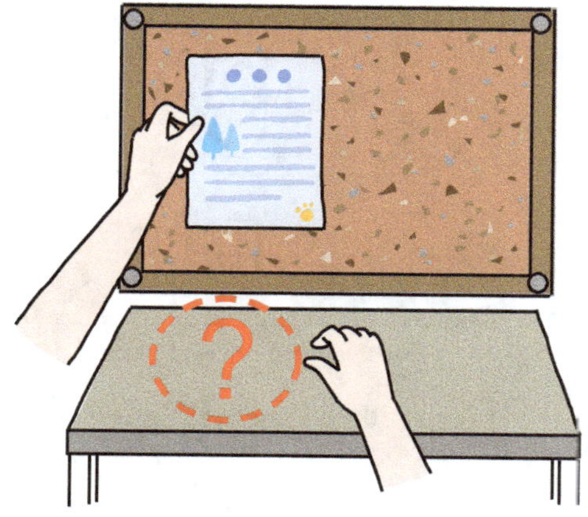

A.	tin
B.	pin
C.	lid

A.	bin
B.	win
C.	tin

A.	kid
B.	dig
C.	fin

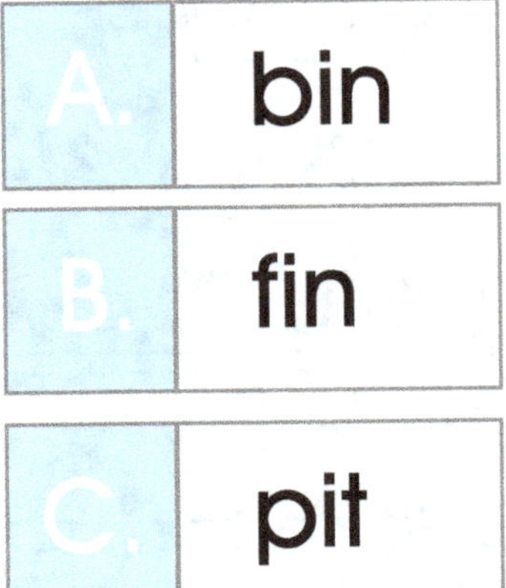

A.	bin
B.	fin
C.	pit

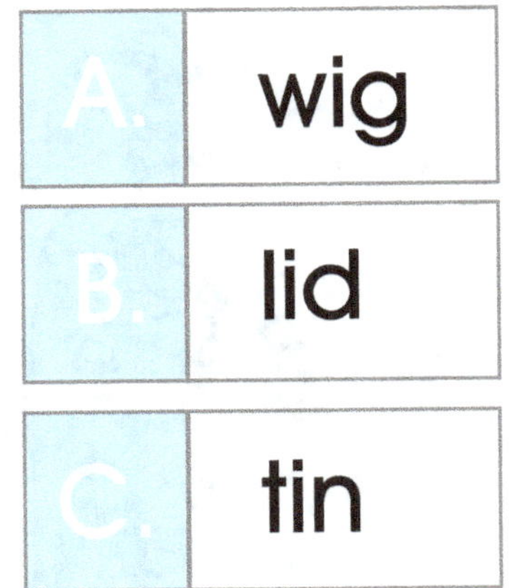

A.	wig
B.	lid
C.	tin

A.	bin
B.	hit
C.	win

Sim and Kim are at the beach.

.1.

Kim prepares some food from a tin.

.2.

She uses the tin to trap the crab.

.3.

The crab hides himself in the pit.

.4.

She spots a pin on the beach. Quickly, she picks it up and throw it into the bin.

When he is playing on the beach, he spots the dorsal fin breaking the surface of the water.

He is surprise when he knows that it is the man with the fin-shaped swimming aid.

A.	kid
B.	bin
C.	lid

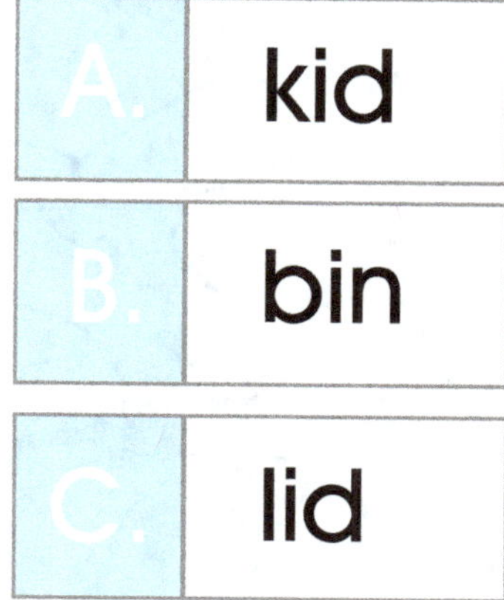

A.	win
B.	fin
C.	lid

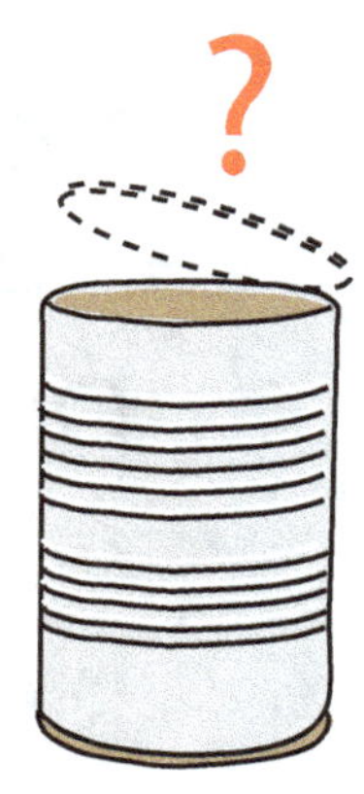

A.	kid
B.	tin
C.	bin

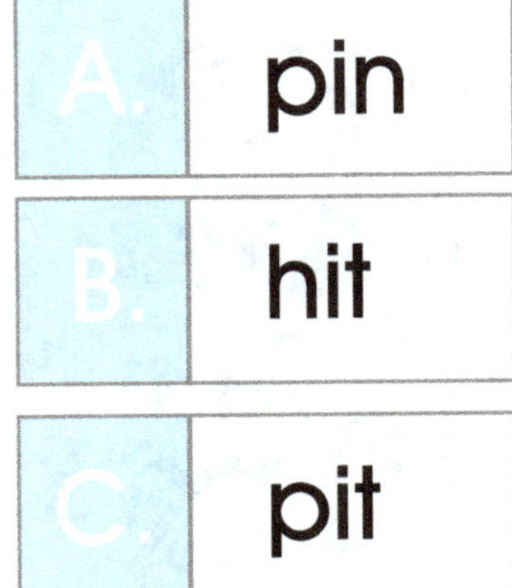

A.	pin
B.	hit
C.	pit

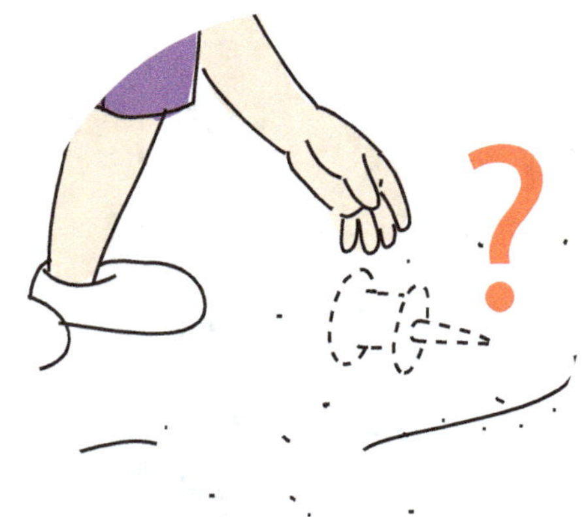

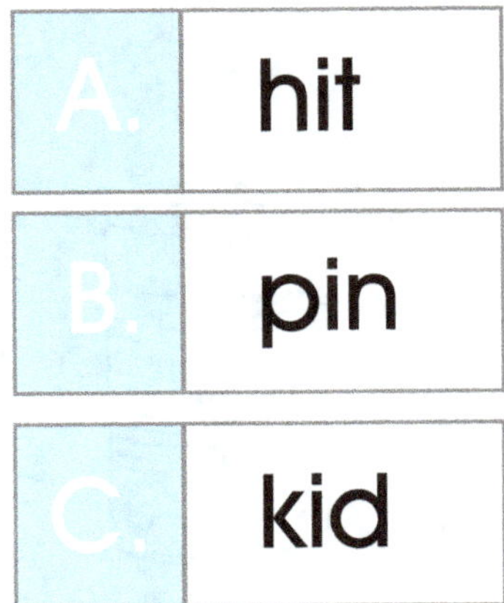

A.	hit
B.	pin
C.	kid

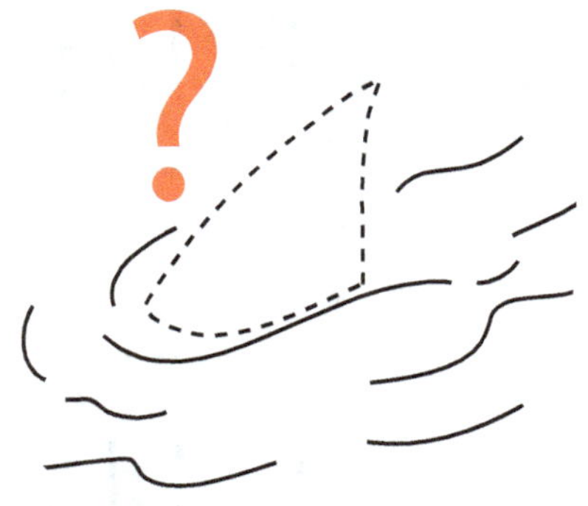

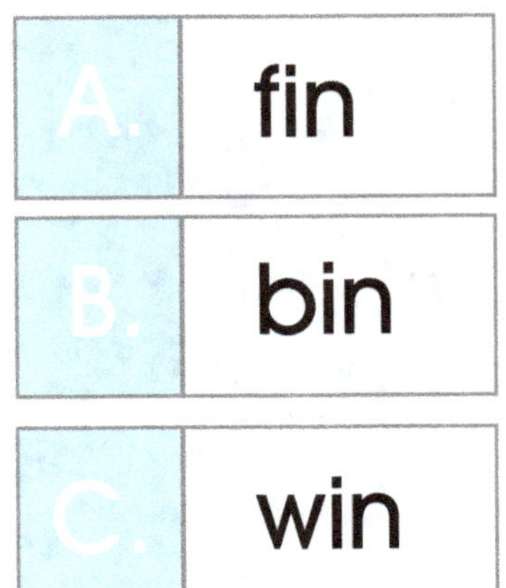

A.	fin
B.	bin
C.	win

a net in a bin

a pen in a tin

an egg in a jug

What is this?

- ( ) This is a tin.
- ( ) This is a fin.

Where is the ring?

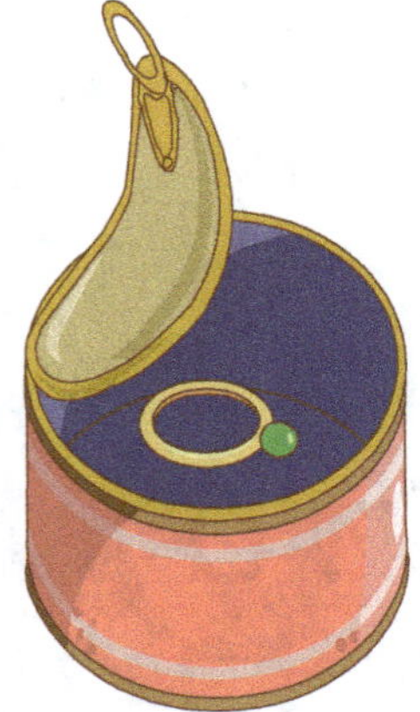

- ( ) The ring is in the tin.
- ( ) The ring is on a bin.

cot

fog

pot

box

log

dog

hot

fox

jog

Join the pictures to the words.

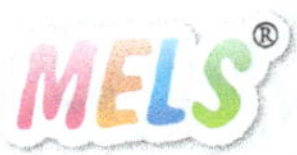

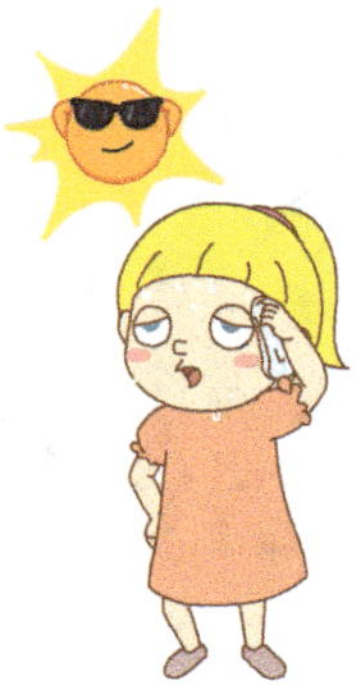

dog

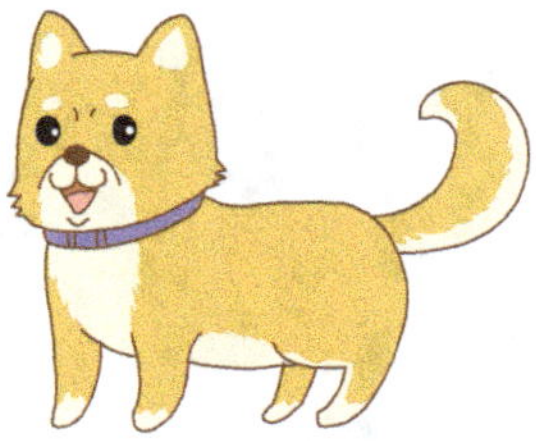

fog

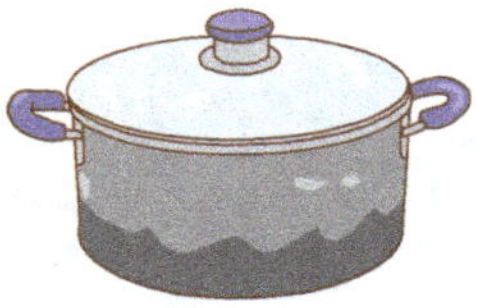

box

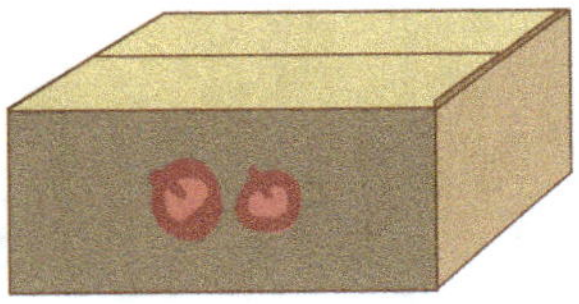

pot

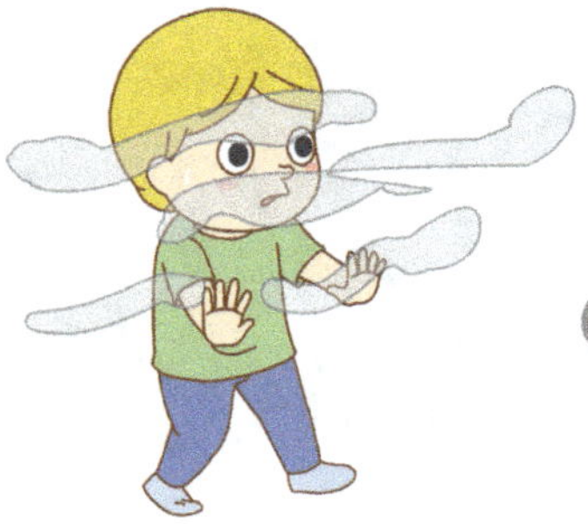

hot

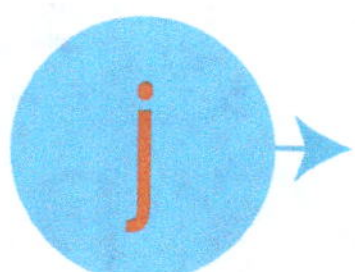
j

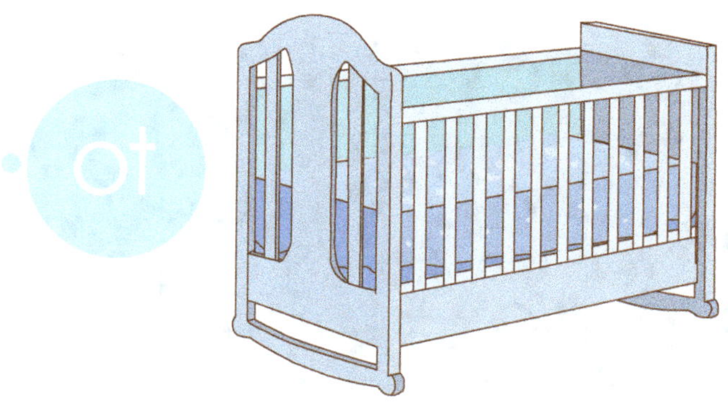
ot

f

ox

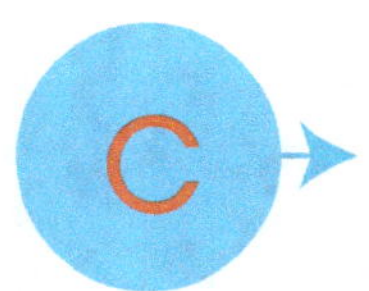
c

og

c	o	t	d	o	t	e	n	o	g
f	o	x	e	n	p	i	n	a	p
h	o	t	l	i	d	l	o	g	n
u	p	o	t	l	o	t	j	o	g
b	o	b	o	x	a	n	f	o	g

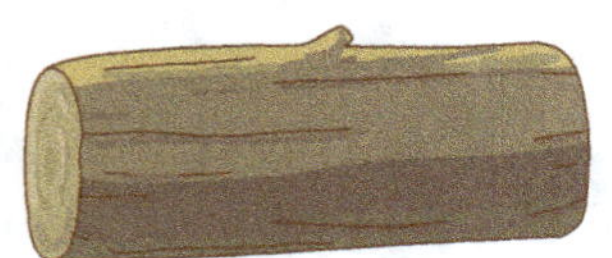

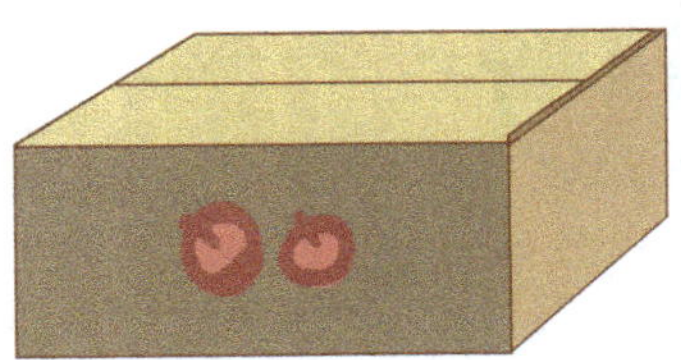

wed

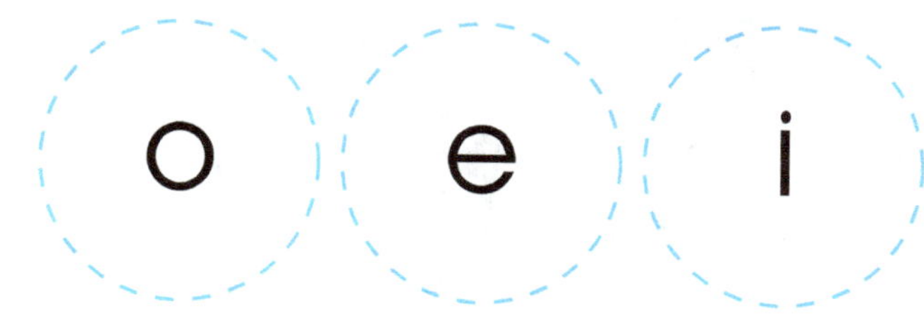
o e i

jog

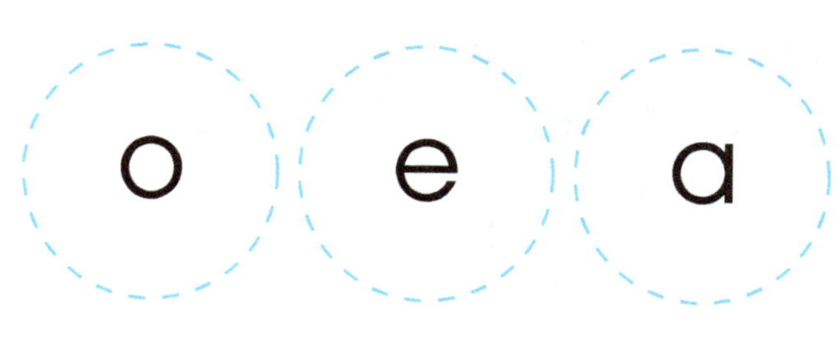
o e a

nap

a i o

win

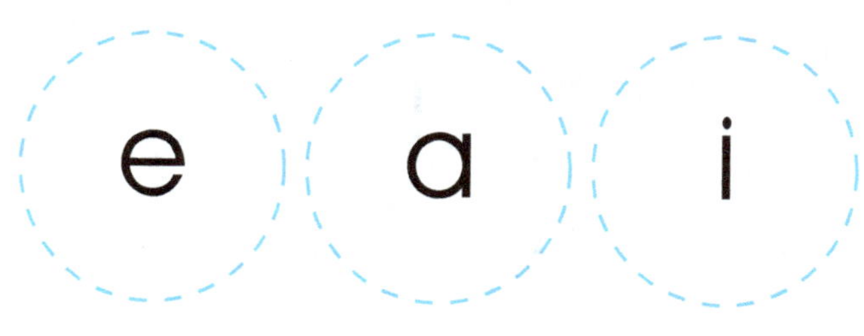
e a i

Colour the letters which represent the *initial* sound of the pictures.

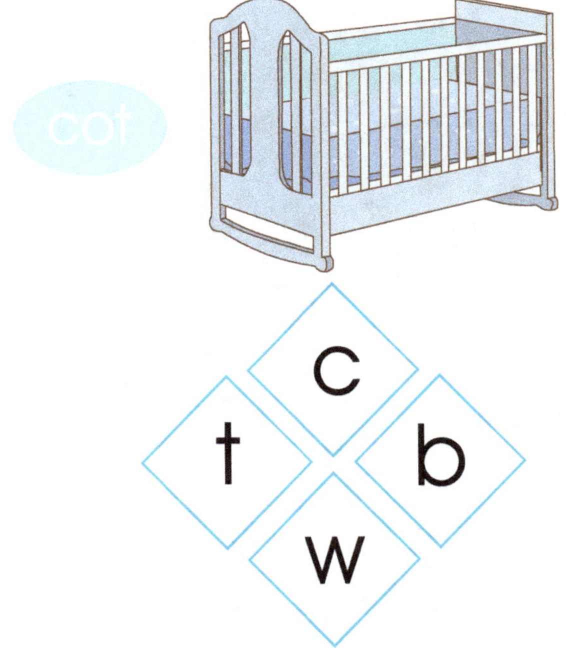

There is a …

A.	hot
B.	cot
C.	log

It is a …

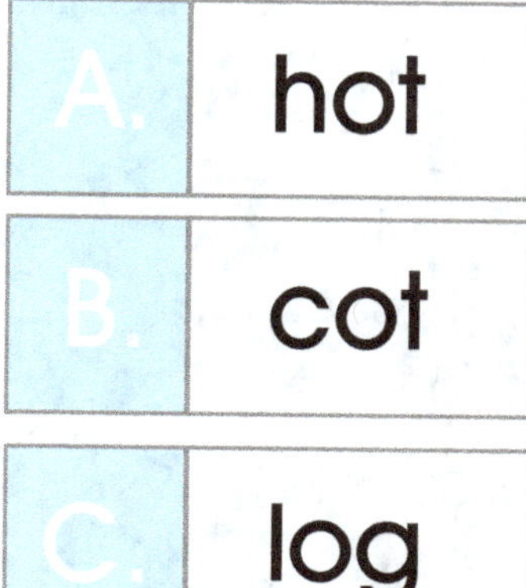

A.	dog
B.	fox
C.	pot

It is cold and full of …

A.	jog
B.	hot
C.	fog

The road is cold and full of heavy ...

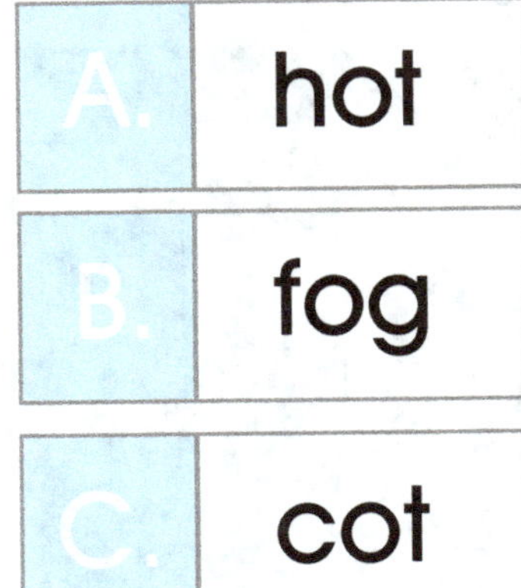

They ...

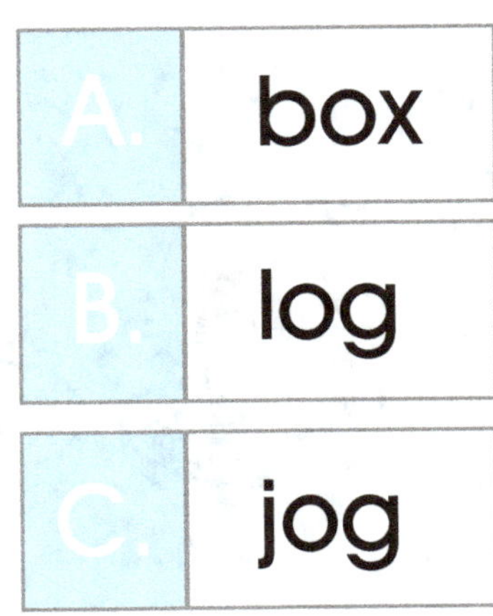

The ...

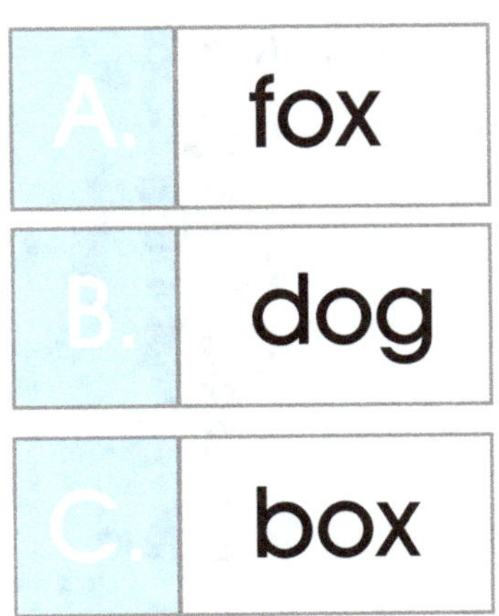

50

The beach is cold and full of heavy fog.

.1.

The fox jumps over the log. It runs around with the dog.

.2.

The boy brings the box from the car. His friend is cooking with the pot.

.3.

They enjoy the food with the fox and the dog.

.4.

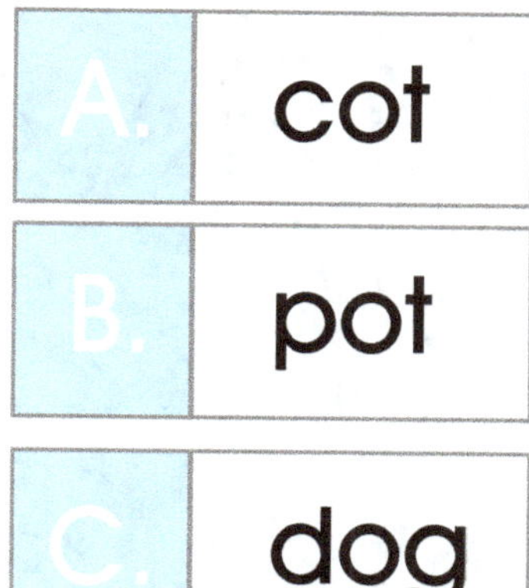

A.	cot
B.	pot
C.	dog

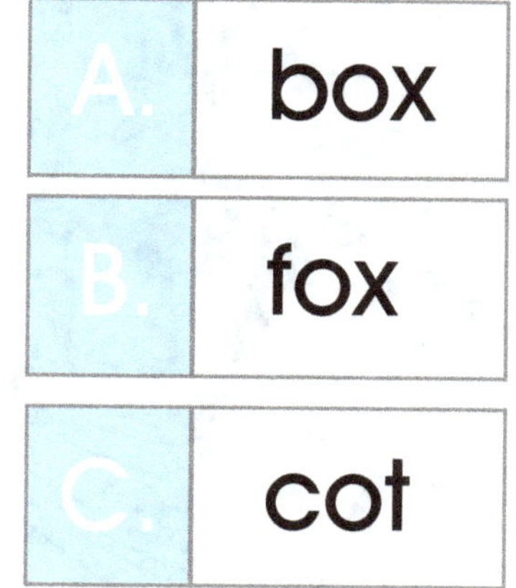

A.	box
B.	fox
C.	cot

A.	dog
B.	hot
C.	fox

A.	fox
B.	log
C.	pot

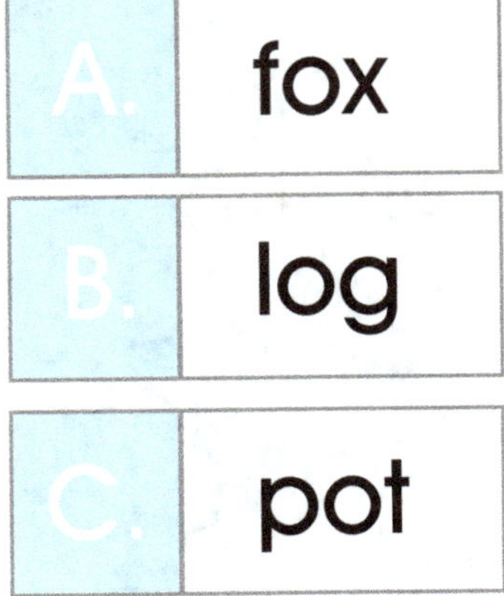

A.	jog
B.	cot
C.	box

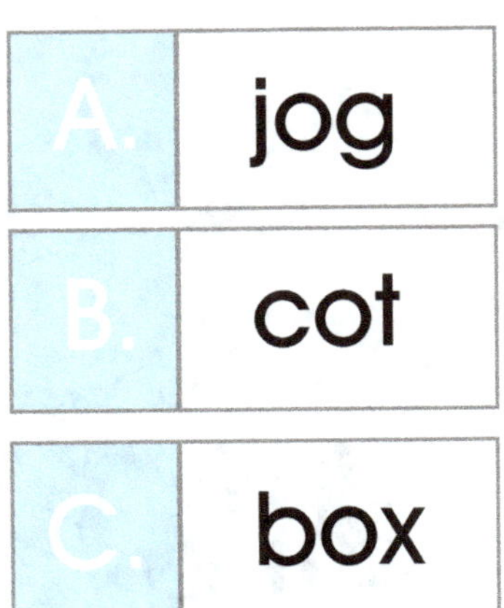

A.	pot
B.	jog
C.	fox

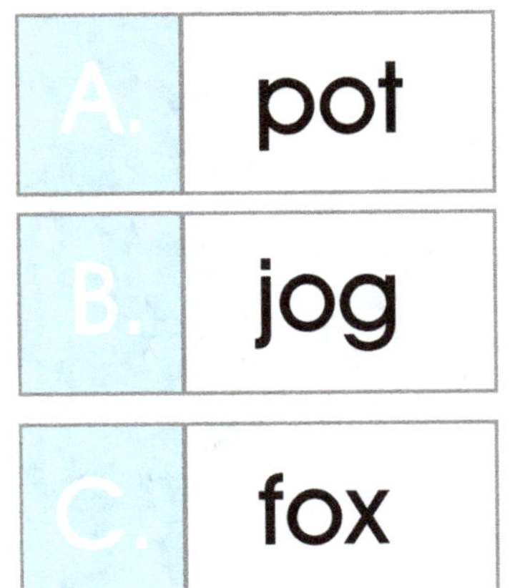

A fox is in a box.

A log is next to a fox.

A dog is under a log.

Where are the dog and the fox?

They are sleeping under the log.

They are sitting on the log.

What are the dog and the fox doing?

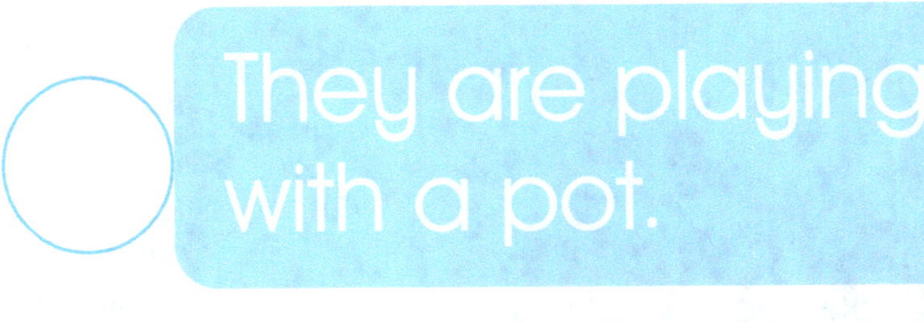

They are playing with a pot.

They are playing with the box.

sun

hut

cub

fun

bun

nut

cut

hug

tub

mud

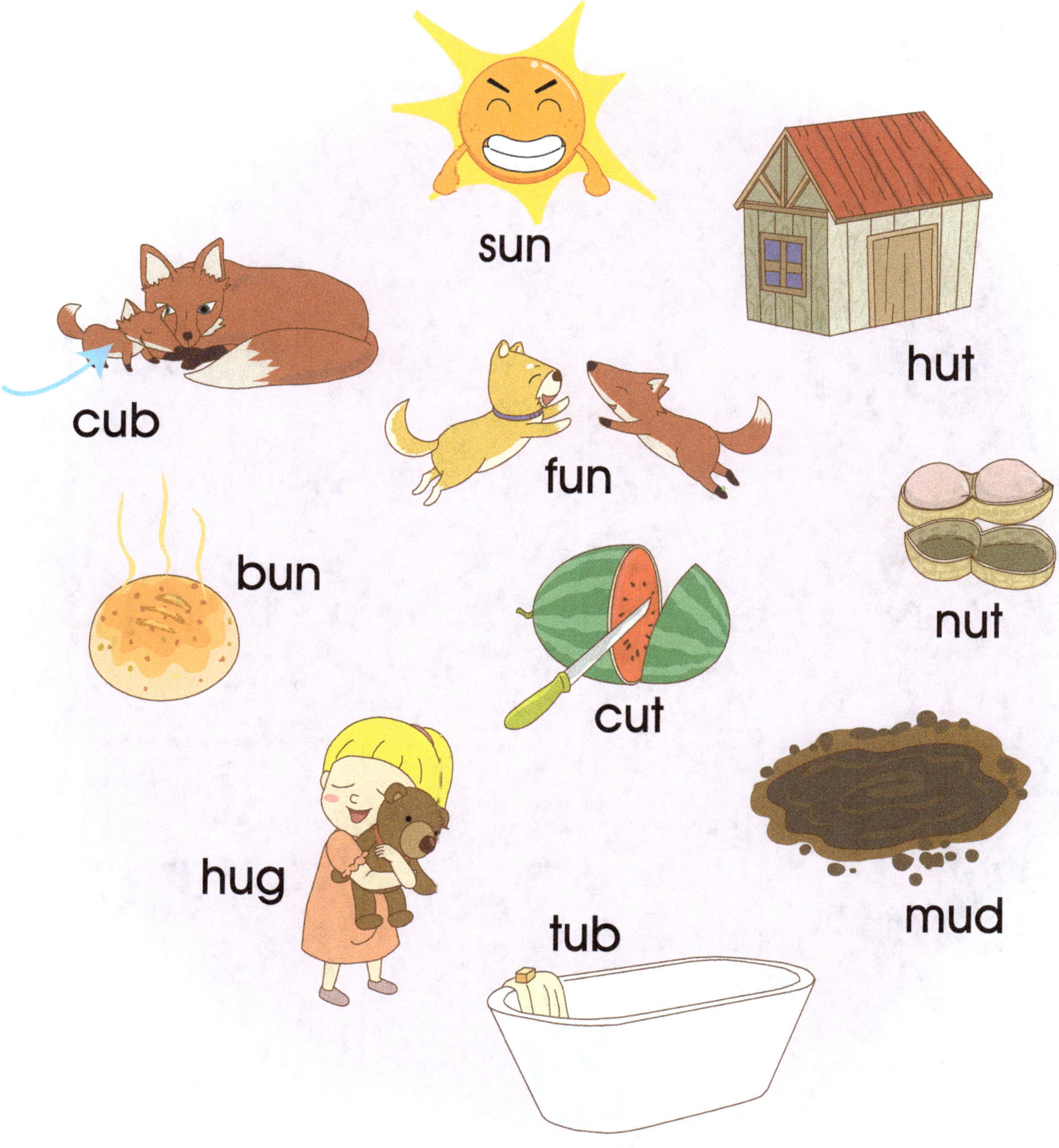

Join the pictures to the words.

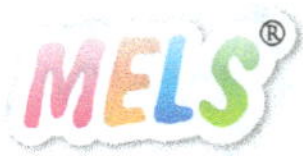

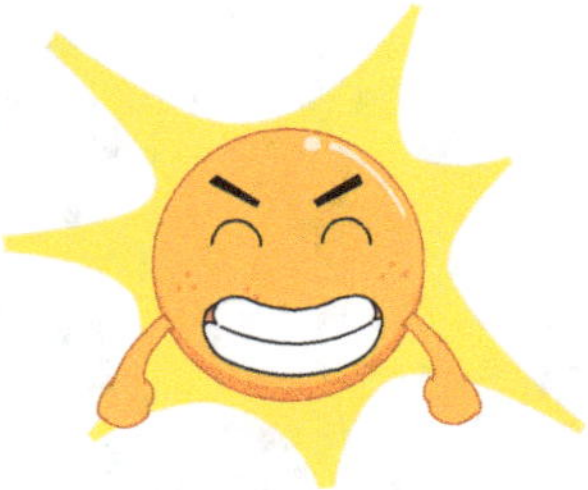

tub

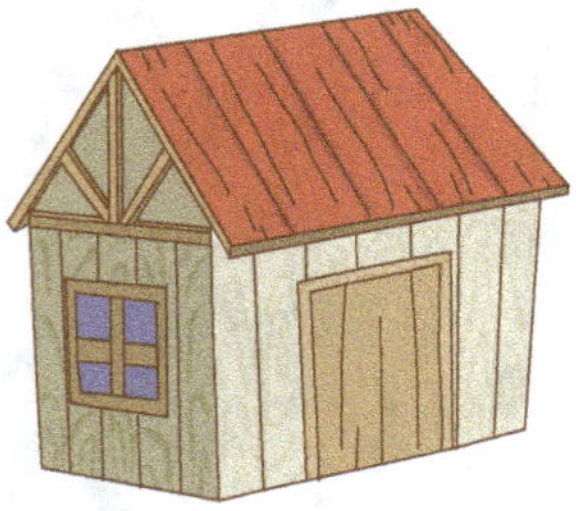

sun

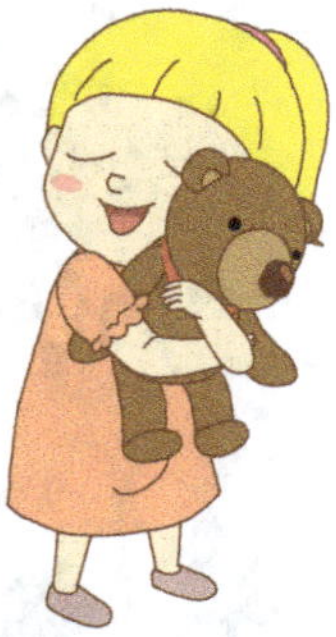

cut

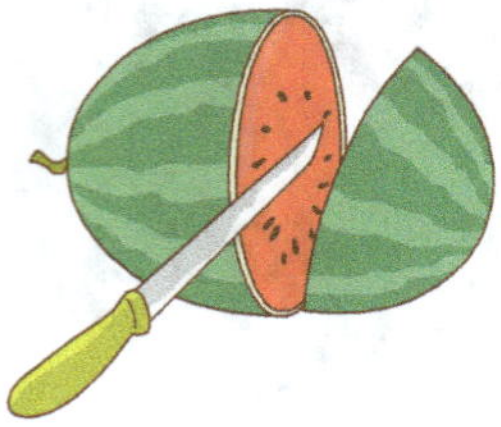

hug

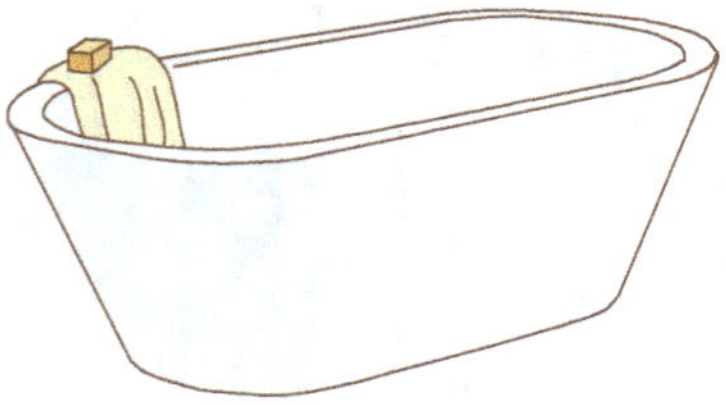

hut

s →

h →

m →

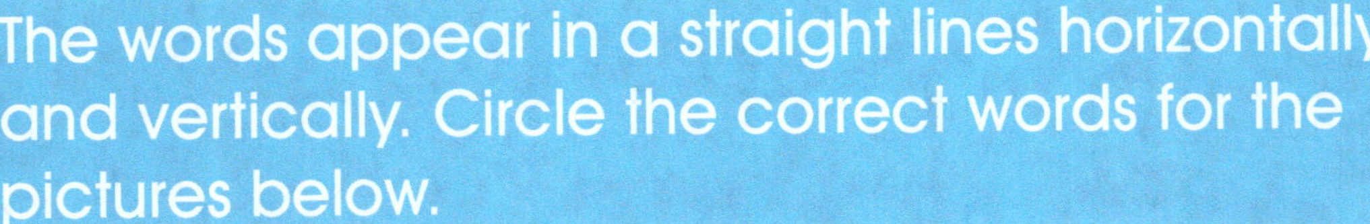

p	a	s	h	u	g
i	c	u	b	a	t
t	u	n	d	l	o
e	t	u	b	i	h
j	a	m	u	d	u
l	o	t	n	u	t

This is a …

Use the knife to …

This is a …

Use the knife to …

This is a …

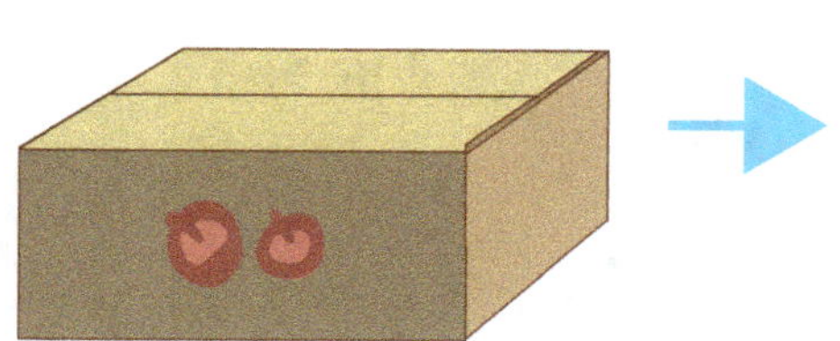

You can take a bath in a …

This is a … 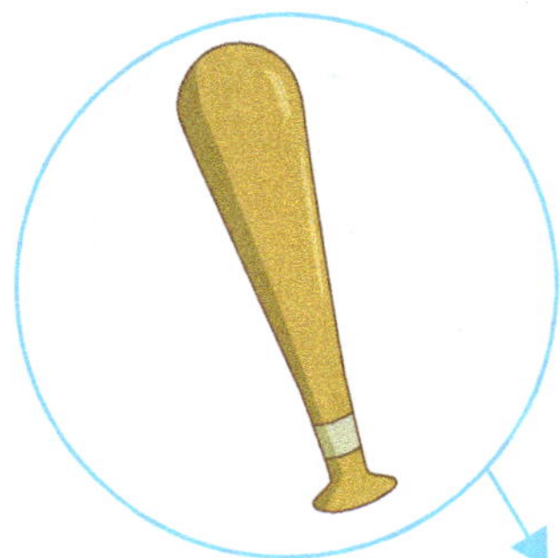

The …

She … 

The … 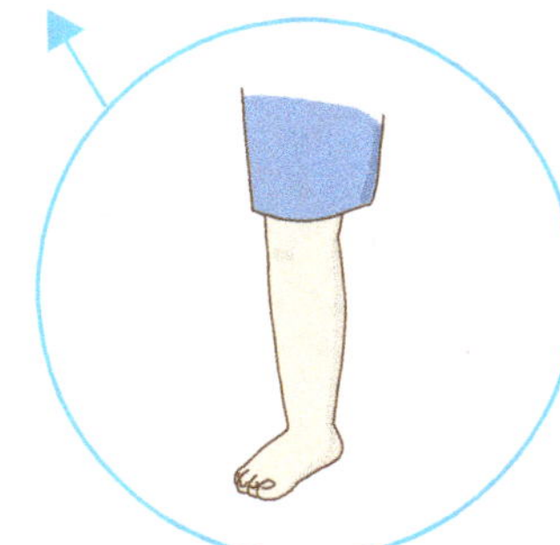

The apple … the cat! 

The … 

The … 

Three … 

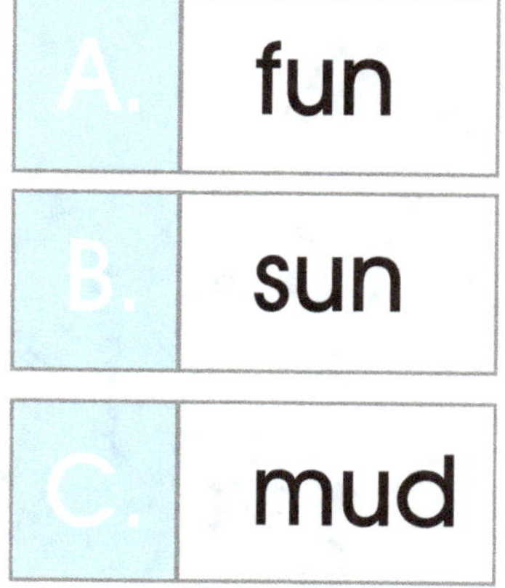

A.	fun
B.	sun
C.	mud

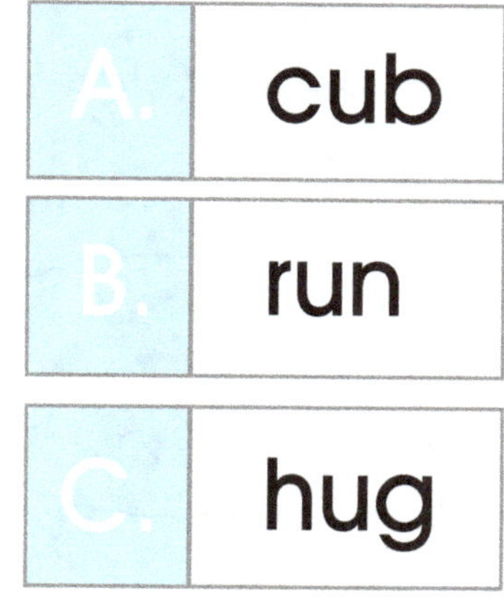

A.	cub
B.	run
C.	hug

A.	nut
B.	fub
C.	hut

He is building a …

A.	mub
B.	hut
C.	nut

He is holding a …

A.	bun
B.	cut
C.	sun

It looks so …

A.	hug
B.	nut
C.	fun

Tut brings some buns from the hut.

.1.

The girl brings some nuts to join Tut.

.2.

.3.

It is hot when the sun is high at noon.

The umbrella provides the shade on the hot and sunny noon.

.4.

Look! The dog is barking at the bug.

.5.

Tut shows the dog the bug is not harmful.

.6.

It is fun to play with the dog.

.7.

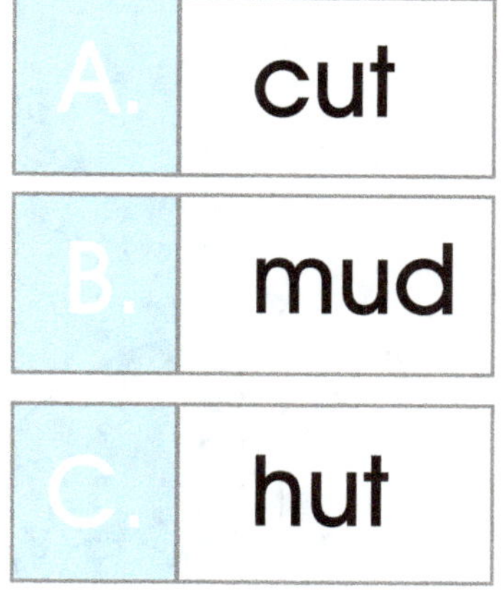

A.	cut
B.	mud
C.	hut

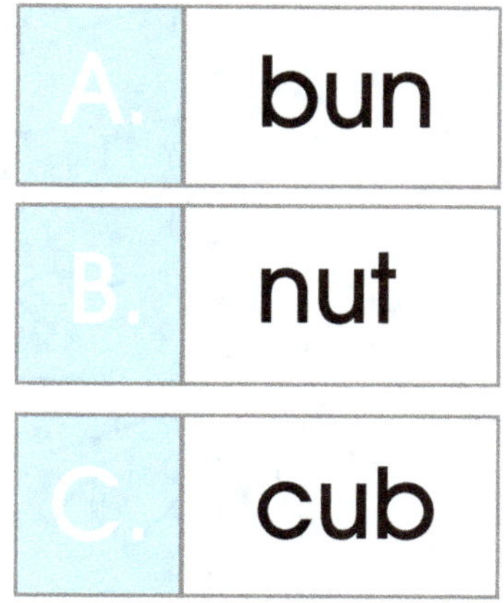

A.	bun
B.	nut
C.	cub

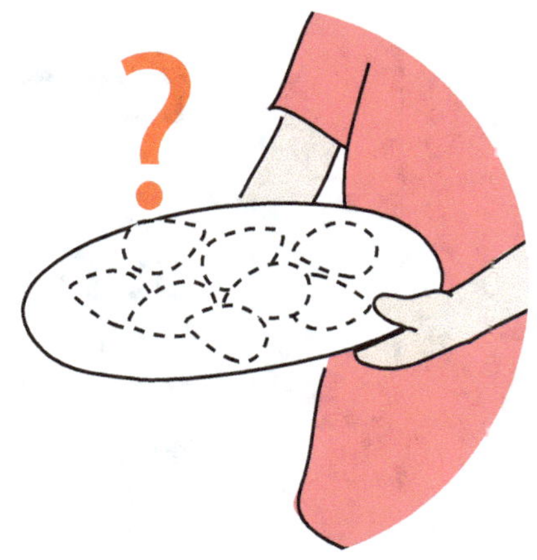

A.	funs
B.	nuts
C.	bun

Based on the story on page 65 & 66, circle the answers.

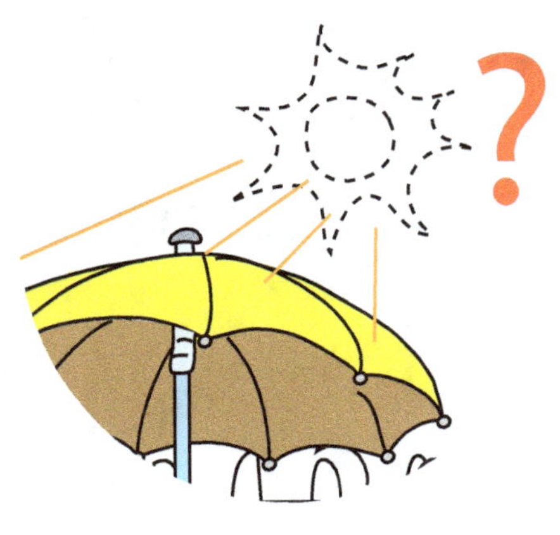

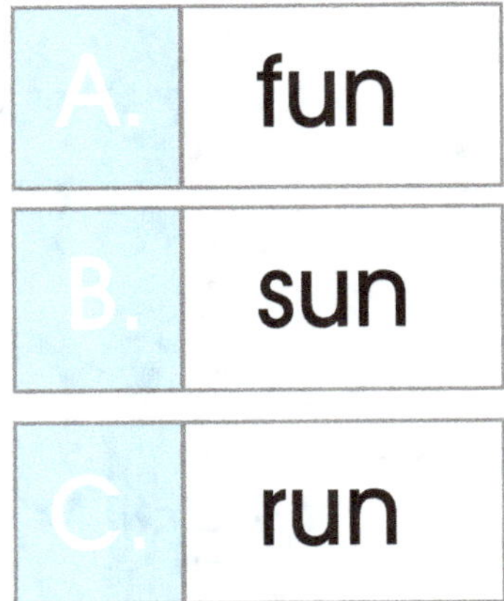

A.	fun
B.	sun
C.	run

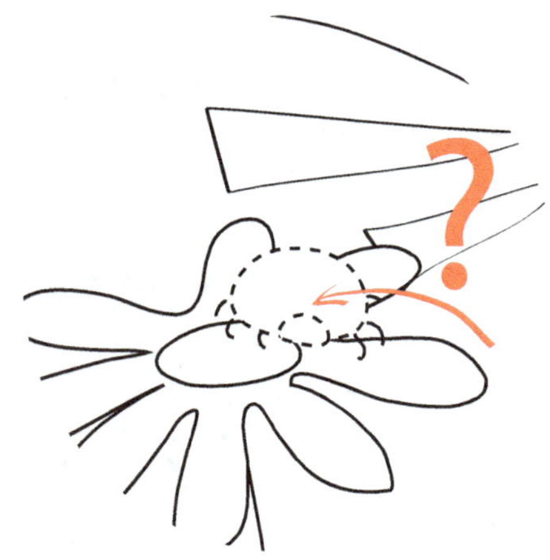

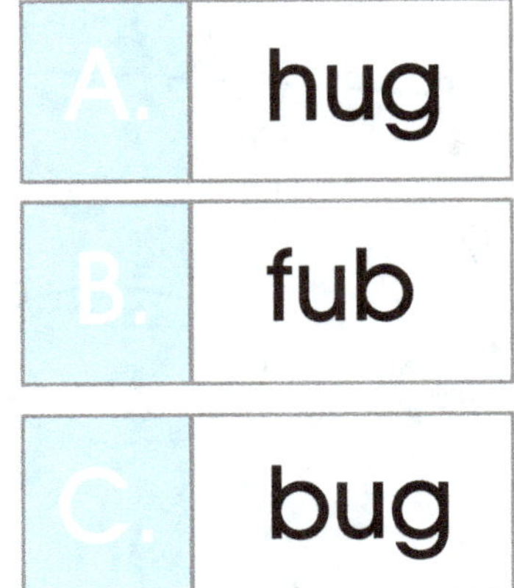

A.	hug
B.	fub
C.	bug

The dog …

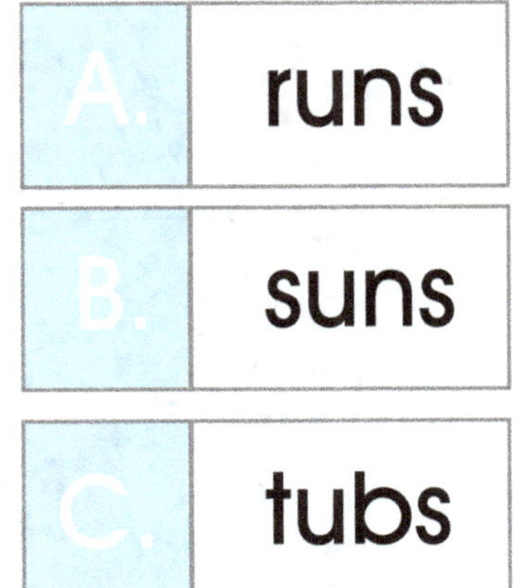

A.	runs
B.	suns
C.	tubs

They like to play in the mud.

They like to play in the rain.

They like to play in the sun.

Where are the dog and the fox?

○ They are in a tub.

○ They are outside a hut.

Are they having fun?

○ Yes, they are.

○ No, they aren't.

www.ingramcontent.com/pod-product-compliance
Lightning Source LLC
Chambersburg PA
CBHW080916160726
48000CB00009B/3005